BOOKS BY NORMA COLE

Mace Hill Remap (Moving Letters Press, 1988)

Metamorphopsia (Potes & Poets Press, 1988)

My Bird Book (Littoral Press, 1991)

Mars (Listening Chamber Editions, 1994)

Catasters (Morning Star Editions 1995–96
Folio Series, collaboration with Jess)

Moira (O Books, 1996)

Contrafact (Potes & Poets Press, 1996)

Stay Songs, for Stanley Whitney (Bill Maynes Gallery, 2001)

Spinoza In Her Youth (Omnidawn Press, 2002)

Burns (Belladonna Books, 2002)

a little a & a (Seeing Eye Books, 2002)

Scout (Krupskaya, 2004)

Do the Monkey (Zasterle Press, 2006)

Collective Memory (Granary Press, 2006)

Natural Light (Libellum, 2008)

TRANSLATIONS BY NORMA COLE

It Then by Danielle Collobert (O Books, 1989)

The Surrealists Look At Art, essays by Aragon,
Breton, Eluard, Soupault, Tzara, edited and translated
with Michael Palmer (Lapis Press, 1990)

*This Story Is Mine: Little Autobiographical Dictionary
of Elegy* by Emmanuel Hocquard (Instress, 1999)

A Discursive Space: Interviews with Jean Daive (Duration Press, 1999)

Crosscut Universe, an anthology of poetry & poetics by contemporary
French writers, editor and translator (Burning Deck, 2000)

Nude by Anne Portugal (Kelsey Street Press, 2001)

Distant Noise by Jean Frémon, with Lydia Davis,
Serge Gavronsky, Cole Swensen (Avec Books, 2003)

Notebooks 1956–1978 by Danielle Collobert (Litmus Press, 2003)

The Spirit God and the Properties of Nitrogen

by Fouad Gabriel Naffah (Post-Apollo Press, 2004)

WHERE SHADOWS WILL

CITY LIGHTS SPOTLIGHT NO. 1

NORMA COLE

WHERE

SHADOWS

WILL

SELECTED

POEMS

1988–2008

CITY LIGHTS

SAN FRANCISCO

CITY LIGHTS SPOTLIGHT

The City Lights Spotlight Series was founded in 2009, and is
edited by Garrett Caples, with the assistance of Maia Ipp.

Library of Congress Cataloging-in-Publication Data
Cole, Norma.
Where shadows will : selected poems,
1988–2008 / Norma Cole.
p. cm.
ISBN 978-0-87286-474-0
I. Title.
PR9199.3.C585W47 2009
811'.54—dc22
2008036995

Spotlight series design by Quemadura
Cover photograph by Jesse Zeifman

All City Lights books are distributed to the trade by
Consortium Book Sales and Distribution: www.cbsd.com

For small press poetry titles by this author and others,
visit Small Press Distribution: www.spdbooks.org

City Lights Books are published at the City Lights Bookstore,
261 Columbus Avenue, San Francisco, CA 94133

www.citylights.com

CONTENTS

WHERE SHADOWS WILL

Imaginations law hits frames
times air delivers to few an aside
so and so also
to speak of these footsteps is
to fear is to be able

Volume is written with straightedge and compass and hydraulics leaving equations of uncharted sex of space and geometry aside instead remap one jeweled curve reassembled encircled sweet mild rainy cold dry windy all the bones save those of theory of possibility

Remain silent enjoyment airs of my heart born of vertices impact stone margin the crown of proportion lodges a smile in the limited path of a thing in a vacuum

Fingertips stapled to a tree trunk don't look down at the lake notes the song to silver in your mouth some moth arbitrarily contriving numbers more bound meteorological assumptions consumed by *delay not*

Fells the higher things international memory of probability and for-
get it sitting by water the moss was moving like animals volumes
gold for smoke all objects show release the leaves clacked together

Is obvious process releasing scent so grew homeless absorbed into
greater supposed detail belief by water now all those stanzaic dots
rock vacancy looking for inevitable spacing by leaf my water senti-
mental several directions I know I've been told

Elements as ridge has foot fools heat up traced out by motion the way
they are all clipped together the fog cool dogeared it spotted with
sparkles of light its heels

Swing like all objects fade away floored from dearth sounds mis-
nomer gully full of restless still mottled by water mumble little inte-
gers their inordinate shadow cools

You have to spit over your left shoulder if you see a magpie trip or waltz or stay within the boulder hemicycle to see where shadows will

Too many arches stuck conditions merely flattened dearly local and then a number of face off first recognition or limbs seniority also had a forked stick of my own turn

That finally detached and walked away trembling too even as things kept moving to gag the breeze of influence in sun this time as the rivers rhyme the usual

Numbers expanded by adjectives hung from trees stop them after a few centuries archers struck shadow kitchens strange waltzes or unmarked generalities replaced by do you know where our letters

Continuing presidents empty gravy presumption and then a number architecturally buttering them beside each other with spaces in between to spit out of the shapes idea

COMMISSARY OF ENLIGHTENMENT!

Numbs together old otherwise
conditions verified dressed and beaten
sit and lie down reliance
understand personally nothing

Was always a little
finishing units

Industrial chunking: two abstract
and one concrete or was it too concrete
and one abstract

That summers versions sweep through torn on vacant tempers care heads made out of wax knock down the house sets afresh a flood of flowers emitting more or less reality sustaining closely free from film and fever few engendered "fair"

Rooms vivid acts in solution as part of the problem founded on cement asleep on principle mind in eye spurs a matter of little sense though learning knowing experience contending for rights mounts the arduous steeps strong money her placed

Fever and glowing gorge speculate immediate delay sweep through

RETURN OF THE SELF FROM LISBON TO SOFA

Human battens smoke to mouth
threatened fretted message

Return of self defying breath
one up against one side mind
one of a nether system of said objects
defy an inspired couch
let alone from it
neither couch sandwich and books
lived and taught to emigrate

A

one box falls out of another box, ashy covenant of separation
two birds, one clamp, no reaction just hanging there as the arrow
     moved
notes put the map back into the water
they don't notice what they're learning
name all the days, parts of them painted to look out of control
     then crashed into a tree
letters in the boxes in the light old lady opportunity
the mirror ceases to be right here, pressure on the hand
     sends a biscuit to the mouth
a circuit connected by eyes stopping watching
quantity of information in the type, nation in the line
     or lines
legs broken and maladroit preview a long corridor filing against
walls engaging hands going without end in the corridor
back to front to quay, cracking of wood, a miner's ladder
     five meters high
notices filled with objects
later, however, a gelatin lit up, Chinese cryptesthesia,
     American music

mural fold or fist, magnetic moment measures behavior, thinking
       penetrates slowly
start over a sensible solution, a compact rower's body zippered
into an orange flight suit, all the confidence of the Chinese navy
       exposing a big area extinct of life forms

C

news flies through the air with a great constriction below
  the throat
false distance puts the teeth back in
the singer reads absence backwards
  resting close
in is by means of a phone in the drawer by the bed
the painting is thinking the weather goes dry and flat
this fold carried by air contains no other object
cat's eye or reflection's midnight in this bed of books
returns things through things
restores things made of paper
  discolored secondary paper
false topography reflecting different intentions
  and starving
both sides of the page at the same time
beautiful and badly made historical documents
faces of wood indicating there's no one at home
  and made not to last
today science will explain everything imperturbable
  contradictory as a credit card

M

that dictionary may be a companion to art but life
       is the most sentimental thing there is
lying around in sub-text hard-pressed to find a resting place
       silence notes its own misreading
tonics of anger, haunted house
the gummed tape is taking a lot longer to remove
       than (we had) anticipated

FORMS OF THE VERB TO MAKE ALMOST ALWAYS INCLUDE THE EYE
for instance the bird is watching the eye or the eye is looking
at the bird
presence of the eye in the text is witness to having done
the other is the stolen eye remembered
the eye is often in the hand
or is provided with a hand
which might introduce light, a double chandelier
permanent, ephemeral, the eye is what touches things

collusion: to doubt is to touch
so the hand supports the eye
being an eye the hand can penetrate line or skin
surface or space
being in the eye
tending towards vision

use: let it be a drawing
being careful
a world without color

sense is opposed to the literal sense hidden in it
figure is description of world with portrait in it
first geometry then portrait

number, space, motion, gift
custom is our nature
by nature so different
numbers imitate space
experience study

He appeared with a large bouquet of roses
and left still holding them
in the tradition of the constellations
gesture detained told the hand
words in no head emended

"written in sand"
material foot where to start
now bend, now turn
so goes the perfume of the rose

as before
hand words
holding speaking
circular

Bark grew up over their faces
nothing prearticulate
people were how they were then
fat or thin
between the words cement, glass, silicone, polymer
banish image

"FREE AS A BIRD"

Yes, says the dedication I exist as a fact
a single
heat dangling outside
difference more visible

as a bite
heat facts are the same
cuticles in ribbons
terms of measurement are not

distract them
distract them to death
so blocking
with raw people

what is natural
persistence is remembered
flares or/are those two
figures trudging up

loudness is a horrible secret
a single dimension beyond imagination
looking sacred doing nothing
perilous reason mopping up

RAVEN

Says I am invisible in my feathers

World knot
young beyond half casual theme
courtoisie & turbulence a few more slowly now
we read little gold suns over the airstrip
no medical treatment for civilians
expeditions *speaking like through a screen door*
peaches for eyes

How faint the spot harmonates unbarred by time, wet and the
shape memory bolted
unobtainable until we learn it

Come up now onto the roof of my mouth and *see* this
shadow that has driven people mad

Common denominators this papers generosity
water's constancy emptied field

what we know passed to the back
mirrors open up another front

"Thou wilt never see that raven again, for I am that raven"

CARDINAL

love's social/intellect —ROBERTO TEJADA, "The Gauntlet"

Born in the ground
obstacles look alike
then action follows
with that piece of bread
while thought set
that piece of bone
and biological nouns
punctuate an awful precision
a pavement doesn't move
"not exempt" and "not above"

BIRD OF PARADISE

calling out very quietly

moving forward
must be her ears
generalizing

left
swept and go behind

to map and to provide

look home

and then

to go

Crosscut universe
get up
assume everything

Lacking sequence
calumnies the rest
then concentrated

Sense circumstances
learning quickly
asymptotic

Sensational
additional power
a landscape "empty"
the scientist, the postman

Mist above a new song
(epic without story)
blood all over the backs of legs

Whose urgency
whose certain point
on certain multiple shadow

Shines
nourished won't dispel
win to it

Mortal set
safety's bounds
IMAGINE

Focus
mountains called
tusk and comb

Discovery of graphite
mouth and after
found adaptor

Double portals
cracked container
never filled

Turn over, turn over
a landscape unit
orbits around opinion

Explicit social
spiral placement
who is public

Light has no emotion
Split breath even light displacement by degrees
Slight breath translates quietly out of event
Into the it

Poems were written over a period of hundreds of years by
the same person. A model of vigor sets up a measure.
An incredible event drives a story. Some are
expectations and what is prior to articulation. The
constant spectral pressure of what's "free about the
rules of objectification, association, "it"'s use, you
put your other in. A kind of reportage they were
getting used to. Was a kind of distraction and took
care of that desire to move around in space, reflection,
enclosure. Exposure, whatever bobs to the surface and
then there's choice, tradition describable like chess.

Describing a chicken or egg, separating it and the way
it is made, intentionally. We named it purpose
purposefully, and how they informed each other. House

eats words, becomes a cartoon. As if it could pick up
the telephone and speak to your expectation, invitation,
somebody's hand, its mark, inside the body. Recording.
Everything outside is X-legitimate. An extra measure.
Why water thought to respond (struggling and breaking)
clever responsible clues involuntarily declared, pretty,
that's resolute.

stones explode.

FROM "MARS"

Now
Makes the sequence didn't know and couldn't know.

set within
rough wing
spread hand

I was hesitant to take the case, having my mind already on another
case

an episode
brightened up
as entitlement
attuned to say

It was customary to broadcast the eulogy to the whole neighborhood,
the immediate environment to absorb the loss.

■

The sun was low over the Indian Ocean, people in the shallow water, a hippopotamus in the water, thick heavy hairless body, large muzzle.

I was on my way from Carthage, it was night. It is not wax I am scorching was dead about her with knots.

do you know
the revealed confusion
of things at a distance
practical as grammar

∎

assured and aroused

Here he wraps the baby up in bark, ties it to his javelin and throws it across the river, out of danger. Camilla grows up a warrior. Wills slant years circling. Watching from this movement enough across the tangle. The river and the person in it.

but all maps are false starts

vested choice
sugar dada
hand in
certain hand

Refusing the war, he turned his back and would not open the gate.
"The wind did it."

VARIATIONS ON SOME OF DANTE'S LAST LINES

And move and hold back
entering by the highroad through the words
and fall like a person hit by sleep
arriving at the place without light

And fall like a dead body falls
and find there the great enemy
and come to a tower all of stones
such that through it the earth opens

We pass between the martyrs and the high walls
even up there water is pouring out
then turning and fording again
sling the noose from the roof of the house

And each and every vapor spent
over winning and not losing
in which it stands caught out
fleet then catapults like a stone

Filling our view
whereupon another valley is revealed

RIPTIDE

There's a shadow over the city
the light, as usual, framing and erasing

Just say you
dream fires each
night smoothing each
collapsing page from

the throat talking
in a series
of measures in
the high desert

the perfect life
in a series
of measured gestures
an invitation to

see the world
from a bridge
that burns in
the next night

WE ADDRESS

... a lead pencil held between thumb and forefinger
of each hand forms a bridge upon which
two struggling figures, "blood all around" ...

I was born in a city between colored wrappers

I was born in a city the color of steam, between two pillars, between pillars and curtains, it was up to me to pull the splinters out of the child's feet

I want to wake up and see you sea green and leaf green, the problem of ripeness. On Monday I wrote it out, grayed out. In that case spirit was terminology

In that case meant all we could do. Very slowly, brighter, difficult and darker. Very bright and slowly. Quietly lions or tigers on a black ground, here the sea is ice, wine is ice

I am in your state now. They compared white with red. So they hung the numbers and colors from upthrusting branches. The problem was light

Our friend arrived unexpectedly dressed in black and taller than we remembered. In the same sky ribbons and scales of bright balance

The problem and its history. Today a rose-colored sky. Greens vary from yellow to brown. Brighter than ink, the supposition tells the omission of an entire color

Which didn't have a musical equivalent. In those days the earth was blue, something to play. A person yearned to be stone

Clearly a lion or sphinx-like shape. The repetition of gesture is reiterated in the movement of ambient light on the windows, curtains, and on the facing wall, the problem

and its green ribbons. The hands almost always meet. Turquoise adrenaline illusions adjacent to memory, to mind. We address

memory, the senses, or pages on a double sheet, classical frontal framing. I want you to wake up now

UNTITLED (FROM *NOSTALGIA*)

I awoke, still chewing something indefinable and sweet —PERPETUA

I awoke, still chewing that one's refusal to know
something indefinable, anything, emotion for instance
and sweet

our hearing

what people will (and)
imagine for each other

at the end of that word, get
ready for it: I turn
to a ladder, Ruby my dear,
with sharp weapons attached to its sides

the lateral motion inflecting difference between riding
and driving her imagination of others' lives

"before ... in time" a satin waistband, the image
of women with eyes closed, "The only

tender" image of when do we eat, and
what book was that

Every bead counts. He has a scratch on his right cheek, she an abrasion
above the corner of her mouth. She wears Treasure A, a lovely touch.
Where does the first person plural begin?

that all experience takes place overboard, what is document? The I'm
telling you form

letters from the bridge

apples, sparely

              telling about

                          overtones

one-for-me

                (observe) in the

                        singing

her work or her tree
"the book of intention": We know it as the name of a book, a writing, a
position, a philosophical legacy, although it was named after a person, a
son, his son killed in battle. Now read it.

ANACOLUTHON

Ecce supervacuus ... —OVID, Tristia

Or you see all of it after all as an accumulation of tone, running, climbing, sliding, the day was burning, we are our day, the ruined fact.

There had been sand in the bed but we made no explanation. We return to the beginning of the organization of the field shaking bits of dried leaf and pine needles out of the blanket.

Picture it one way, then listen closely, there are no apples here, something that reads together shall invade the separate parts of the mind.

We discovered it, why not dance on it? We discovered its sightlessness, the streets clogged with concerns, with a kind of proliferation like mange clogging the intersections and creating a labyrinth blotting out all light, careful reader.

After all, the first images were a name and a house without the frame, and the woman had four eyes, it's part of the unities, an invention that changes

As we sing memory, memory, over and over, again as before, these piles of cypress burnt not for content but rather a question of spelling.

HER AND THERE

"Consciousness," explained More Pataphysics, rigid with emotion. The weather turned. We had not heard you come in. "Have you ever forced a lover out of your own dream? Why can't I write a book called *Fraud*? They talked about the music as it forms, far away in time, in a state of place, in all its versions. She shook until she split the mirrored room. She shook the map-case open, terribly and ruthlessly. An ocean or continent of blood poured out in sheets on the body.

CONDITIONS MARITIMES

THE TEXT IS SHAPED AFTER
the letter of the ocean

THIS SHAPE ONCE REFLECTED
becomes its own narration

The fragmentary teeth become the
allegory of completion

There she stood, dressed like a sailor
in black pants, striped jersey, pea jacket

Wearing amber for luck
and company

"into eventual accuracy" (Michael Ondaatje)

Inverted lives
it was said refer to the ocean

There she stood, etc.

Thus the false map is scrawled
by sleep as if history assembled
these names

This time and its history a calculus of stars, the limit of
the formal plain, its proportions

                                 the sign for division
outside its context

                    its issues' decision

(soon we would begin to lose
the feeling in our fingertips)

                that it was science; that it was so
appealing; that rules are the instrument

Here we are talking about the playful
handling of an object
the negotiation with an imagined acceptable

That the poem is a toy
with the structure of insomnia

That gardens being lit thus saved
just to know and not have
in local practice
given up that control
"in your dreams"

That time, that spiral marrow
(the space between shoulder blades)
that hyphen without reason
lashed to death by virtue=reason=virtue
(the reason between knowledge and fact)

I   wash my feet
before going to bed
contrafact: one complete thought

"I SAW SHELLS ...

... that were bigger than I was."
—JOURNALIST, Chechnya, 8 March, 1995

Rhythms are precise, the
intervals approximate

Night, passacaglia
black butterflies
in front of the sun
killing memory

Night is scored for
soldiers' mothers
come in trains to take
them home

Worldstruck, with an instrument
night, gift and theft

M FOR *MOIRA*

and the lobster, viz. Dante there will always be an-
other note to sing. that conversation was about the translation and
what was inside. forgotten is the other speaker now, "a foreigner," his
proposition of *idleness* the house unswept, transitional

the classical poet who speculates about desire and
the tides, the romantic painter, the most obvious one to whom one
might refer, the ease with which one forgets mornings are not what
they used to be. there is a gloss one might refer to at some other time

but for now the morning paper is arriving *heralded
by a barking dog* the woman in water is the usual waking dream *hors*
lucidity. you may not ring. add the first person creates rings around
the story, but you are already familiar

with all the references except perhaps the odd
dream or old syntax, and these two photographs I'd forgotten to send
from the Hill of Mystery, i.e. Carthage; the conversation about the
light is traditional. since one lives in letters small enough to fit into
lenses specifically ground

to unscramble every anagram, it could just as easily have been a bathrobe or ballgown, Paris or port. but whatever one was under, finally, the pavement, do you not recall your earliest memory

or anecdote become my memory: "That was the last time I ever signed my name." tomorrow you will spend at the office of the Board of Supervisors. *Now the tape please.* the music stands in for the rest and perhaps you recognize the metamorphic repetition

seasons outside the range of days, shadows are literal, one rescues another from a shooting car or rockets dropped from flying carpets. look at the weather. it's the new year so have some honey,

: METHOD

a story traced between two points
beneath which a line was drawn
sitting in the place of words

Dropping stitches
Night by night
A measure
Where the sky is striped

Learning to read: moving proof
of its fictional space: first it reads
laterally: things are the
consequence of names: do not
inquire into the meaning
of speech: you like it
clearly: addressing it while
speaking it: the implications

woven from what it encounters:
still in the heat or greeting
impulse: dressed between
two pages: things we see
in our sleep

: WELL

Eating and shitting pearls, we
tell each other stories, listening for difference

A starfish sits on your foot, an effect of fog in London
or Paris

There is a thin film of dust on the leaves. We
eat this dust

Life is eclipsed by work, an island of fire in the
burning sea, consolation of desire

The invisibilities would live inside the well
dropping their arms

"with such grace"

"As for sleep"
untimely in our summer home

the space refuses rationalization

THEY FLATTER ALMOST RECOGNIZE

FOR BEN E. WATKINS

1

They flatter almost recognize their white shadows. Ecliptic conjunction: I would print it myself if I knew how. As it is, the point of view: once in the days of my youth: in those days the room stood still: prose and rest. A table-like structure. The picture completed itself in shadow on the wall.

2

A past event has been converted into prognostication: "I saw the sky, some stars and a few leaves. . . ." Jean-Jacques Rousseau, *Reveries of the Solitary Walker*. Predicated upon an unprecedented lack of experience. Its shimmering surface at eye level appears to float. There was nothing off his face. The picture completed itself by definition.

3

Words or notes take this pre-existing form and arrange themselves to or against or around it. Or a formal fact applies itself to experience. As you see, all counterfeit in some way. Its thickness, or rather, its incalculable thinness ungraspable. The picture remains incomplete.

4

He says he's not alone, since he has to build the neck around which the necklace will fasten. Here is the nature of my question: answer me "son of water, scammony, cubeb," *delerium linguae*. The darkhaired child must have been a phantom, since we had not got word of her. Then came a progression of pictures.

5

An open color in the Rif, night was a mirage that might be sung. "May you awake to goodness" is another. Contrafact a piece of time, what by its nature is restraint or demands restraint. Beyond estimation, it is a proposal, but a proposition of whatever. Looking, you experience as experience the refusal of experience.

6

Line, screen, a smoke-screen, a double-paned glass muffling what passes back and forth in a piece of time, the spectral pattern: woman, city, book. The foreseeable future. Of the possibility of certainty, of experience. The illusion of progress is partitioned here. Pictured here.

7

Walking, I am walk? Science, you undergo but never have: that is, the material charts: her head rests upon the desk, upon the open book. We are remembering sound. Of the——— between experience and the experiment. In this use, the *lacuna* of the proposition is physical, concrete, and non-verbal. They enter from the wings.

THE SONG OF THE SEA DOGS

Local disaster had barred a spiral
shadow forms a bridge
it rained that day, the
day I fell out the window
I foresaw a new shape
for the galaxy

The binding and stakes at the helm
bilge water and the cisterns of
drinking water, skids or rafts
to transport the elephants
after all, or above all
why did the angels fall?

She became a bear and gave
birth to a son
he was placed there and also
the scorpion who killed him

ALLEGORY FOUR

To start looking immediately
forms of deceit foregrounded
to keep from falling
inside the pressure of things
nailed by the other
the empty frame "and sex"

Familiar mimosa
follows her sailing patient proof
differences mainly in quartertones
the mirror dominated the room
movement where there was none
recapitulation of things you can hold up to the light

Into the mind that walks
deductible pleasure in the records
chained to the tracks
whistles "tied to the tracks"
that there would always be breaks
the things was caused by sound

Can it be changed
and would it be useful to change it
letters big idea in the frost
experience makes its categories
red filter for what happens in the woods
in time opens the dictionary

ALLEGORY FOUR

Going back to the fire
adjacent and constructed
bandit of enunciation
that's what I do
consciousness has to have an object
the second time through

That it's his baby
there had been an extra separateness
overall, a wedge of illusory protection
its triumph—no words for it
here, instead
useful measure

Individual memories
of course there are others involved
or there will be
the stern for the ship
if you can lie in it
tables into scales

Sit down and write a symbolist
direction of motion
he likes lists
somewhere that's where
a piece of charcoal on the floor
or thread furling a sail

ALLEGORY SIX

Adrift intend
it's a picture
but what it's of
the address can locate
reliving their hours of agony, assignment
to live away from that

The elements and an other
one of the few mutilated copies
the silent or invisible point of reflection
not "a person" to hear
all of our performing selves
arms around each others' waists

All the old stories were trivial
I think I'll stand on my head
live upside down, by gravity
reluctance to turn the page
then horses, tigers, train tracks
on spectral streets

The spectral lion crossed my path
its pertinence complete or absolute
and so is the instead of
reassembling against stepped notes
philosophy of shortage
chronology to the source

ALLEGORY TEN

The purple dappled man
a living plurality
anchored in reality
reading stratagem again
quasi-journalistic
the either / or part of the brain

Fighting at the temple
become a lodger there
how all the sounds are
"action potential"
the language's name
natural electricity

Superhero for a day
hot wires run through
wires imitating light
twitch as though attached
and sound scans
the way memory is not local

Shatters the big picture
chipping eccentric permission
humming "too young to die"
where luck might laugh
erecting iris flags
we remember you this way

ALLEGORY FOURTEEN

The dream is already vague
because of calls that
require you to sleep suddenly
and abruptly each night
"more light" mistakenly
beaming into false soliloquy

Or was it false light
hanging over the main room
its inner spatial language
implicate error
reconciled by every tense
speaking everything in retrospect

By consideration of our
national stone or anticipation
of our building an idea of it
has been changing eventually
the definitions will change our
experience shifts what we

Think to be circumspect
isolating what we think
the margins are deliberate
progressing from verb to verb
the gate speaks across the square
the changing light speaks for itself

THE FIGURE OF THE CHILD AT REST

Water ripples through the page. A discernable face is in the page. Working steadily, you read like a doctor, but what kind of doctor "likes it but doesn't want to have it"? I am always repeating myself.

Enclosed by land or time, this singing is trapped. A door slides open above a cliff. Or shut. For some, each act is final. Or infinite revival. See note on existence.

The mere bodily pressure of a person. "Idleness, idleness," he said. "Emptiness," she said. "Purist," he said. I had been looking for the person in this city, in this house. Ill-kept, we are always a different person.

OF HUMAN BODIES

Here the subject thinks "there could be flowers" or "the water was a bit disturbed when the ring fell in." All that, painted from said things, pleases it. That explains all things except Ovid's exile which we will probably never understand. That adds to our sense of fragility, confirms the order in which we read. You still have the right to bear arms, "thing and joy," the *anxious doubt* that was once written about.

There are several versions of the story where she is transformed into a swallow, flies around a pillar.

And do you find the rhyme? It originally meant spoken, the sentence, but spoken. Flight, interchangeable with fate. As for myself, I can't begin to approach the woods with it. The words of its condition.

DECIR:

yo soy la luʒ (ESPIRITUALE)

The whole story of the light, as the unsaid name is or bears its declaration: pandemonium. They used to say that an amenable place would cure you or undo you.

A woman has been drugged, then lowered into the tank on a rope around her trunk. We do not see the margins of the aquarium or the water but we understand she is in water by the way her hair and long skirt swirl about her. The transplant is a kind of representation intended to facilitate understanding. In order to see the plants outside experience. Identity is inside the body of the letter. Struggle is not presentable.

Extremes do not average out. Elaboration of the correction: I was the hour, etc. They do not cancel each other out the way statistics have predicted. About choice, "if only" reinforces (an idea) by confirming the projection. Occasions are on-the-spot assumptions where optical function solves problems while you sleep, "heart in mouth."

DEL TEMPO FELICE

"No greater grief . . ." etc. Meet me at the retroactive vision and frag-
ments come out. In this institutional setting, I accidentally spill wa-
ter into your lap. Once ordered, events are as vivid as on the screen.
The verb forms a halo of error like force, or is force, and like the two
crossed fingers holding an object between them in a caress on a con-
tagious field, it builds around its own order. Construct a practical
grid for it.

People gather at the center. He pretends to introduce objects into his
mouth. They are unafraid to enter such a dark place. Seeing the word
come into being, gradually, letter by letter: if a chain of introduction
made itself clear, behaved like an incident. And if there were none,
give me a bed.

Sleep is an open ticket. The circumstance in which women wear the
underpants of men remain undocumented. I tell you, it's purely
practical. The trip was through the lake and the lake was in the heart.
"Oh, the light. I had quite forgotten."

HE DREAMS OF ME

as Don Quixote who has many beautiful daughters. In love with fear itself. Design problems move. Survival means in each case not to resist the movement or where one is in it. "It's the world we make." It's similarity just in name. There is a word for this representation of an unswept floor.

A little of life simply escapes from a shallow dish, a secret gift. It often begins on a small island which eventually attaches itself to the mainland. Up and up—the challenge of masking boundaries. See that high water mark? It's white paint or what music expects from polyhymnea.

A new season. Flesh and power, not a thought. The letters were erased from their skin, the name folded, the single word "will" encircled. The internal quality of the smoke that dances, the hard external body, many painters painting time, the cabin in the mind. Magic resonance imaging put folds in the page.

Amber in silver. Calculate the strength of the dead. Becoming an extension of that pattern in the iron curtain already forgotten, she has lost a lot of ink. There are bumps in the air, collisions with obstructions revealed only by the shapes around them, actions such as watering or reading, repeating or arriving. "Half my days" and then the other half, etc. High water mark, red quartzite, red osier, sumac, fire opals seen at dusk. Fear of strange places as the fear of not being able to find the way out.

SUMOUD

Once I saw a bride standing in the sand....
—JEAN SAID MAKDISI, *Beirut Fragments*

Dust on the scales. A smith beating time on an anvil. Rehearsal of the city-state.

The idea was not to leave. Strands of my hair stick to your face, a steeply-tiered interior with freshwater areas at the bottom. To write was to release meaning, concentration could mean resistance.

A stranger of mine, he spilled his drink. I took it as a sign. My village was erased from the map.

One crosses the road by the port. After the journey, warm bread covered with thyme and olive oil.

Undo the rules of the game, the green line which is the crossing. Children are tied to their beds so they can't step on the shattered glass in their bare feet.

Turns back the information, a field of colored knots. No summary at all points. Choice or the illusion of choice. The good news, he's not going blind.

at some point, or at gunpoint
human is to wander

the light is not the usual light
the birds are

just the naked man and children playing outside, the dangerous current and threatening silhouette, damp spots and dried crusts on the blankets. the star man's flesh eventually tracks to the plush red cut-velvet wallpaper in a hotel in New Orleans that had once been a brothel featured in a nostalgic french film whose sound track was a keening behind the cracking of knuckles

ESTAR FOR HÉLIO OITICICA

They wore strips of fire along their limbs for that death dance, fabric striped like roof tiles, a cabin in Eden, small stars in the shape of proverbs

Checks and balances her thoughts myself, organdy or tulle crumpled and bunched around a rolled core of burlap upon a reflective cylindrical horizontal base

The shorn wrapped woman opens the glass *bólide*. Rose pigment. Floral pattern on the one hand, cape on the other. Overlay

He wanted to emphasize the other box too. In order to do this, he needed Milton. His friend had died in the sea

He needed to celebrate the bandit, Lycidas. The top of the box held between two hands, diagonal slash a lighter gray across the lid

The open box above, small abstractions piled inside. Another lighter smaller object to the right and on the following page

Space relief underneath, the slanted opaque illusionary planes on metal stands. On glass. Two round objects seen from the side, urn-like, from above, sphincter-like, pebbled

At least four kinds of cloth from white to dark, a striped one with a sheen to it. Held, smiling above the gravel and the shadowed grass of Eden

borrowed nature, neighborhood

dated by experience
                "I'll kill that bitch"
She escapes into the margins
      by walking with
her vacuum cleaner

time fills up is a
way of accounting for

longing for experience, records it
as if it were not, district, zone

There is a narrow band of shadow
down the center of a single page. Deliberate

a particular clarity lends itself

UNCLE HARRY'S ANTIBODIES

how people use each other like serotonin
linked by formaldehyde to protein
the antibodies will find you

if you hear hoof-beats
they must be zebras. Ils sont très sensibles à
la motion – it's motion they notice

his license plate said For
your information I am very
creative I am a voyeur
I like to watch women piss

motion moving moves
water and a line of type

While they invite you into the
books in their titled cages tumble

Out you were being scrutinized or they
do no interest here who measure

The proverbial or the inevitable
fly still in her hair, the suggestion

Of movement: pulled the glass of milk
toward herself by a string

She had tied around it, what
is singular, milk running into

The gutter, the speaker is still
and lit. Sail on, she said

Arresting song, she wrote into the dark
light proves as eerie as real life

FOR CECILIA VICUÑIA

FROM "SPINOZA IN HER YOUTH"

^^^

Today I went to visit the
ancient world, a world
of glass constructed once
then unconstructed, it
bypassed quality, so I came
home and read music what
a woman carries a tune for
instance decentralization
is centrally planned and
can be revoked at any time
it's noon. The moon
is out, I'll meet you
by the pyramid
^^^

^^^

Mount Rubbish where the light must make its way through fire
Let's make this page into an apartment, an enlightenment structure like
being inside someone's skull. Over to the right there's a red car. To-
gether they had planted that tree I enjoy to see you notice
They called it The Colonnade although there were no columns visible

∧∧∧

∧∧∧

Objectivity and brother Chance
excuses locked in their randy dance
blood flowing from elbow and foot

We knew the place. It was
a crossroads. Tolls were collected there. Eventually we burned our
houses and bridges behind us. They erected a temple. Nothing from
that time is visible now except for the ruined baths facing the river
and the reconstructed amphitheater on the eastern slopes.

street of the heart and
the street crossing it

The city was a quarry, then a fortress.
After his conversion he built a great cathedral on the island. Burnt to
the ground. Its foundations were found. Its situation on the river, its
advantage, proved to be its undoing. They met no resistance. We
kept the language.

gypsum, limestone, sandstone, sand

A POET ENTERS THE BODY OF EXPECTATION

It could have been me for instance using a word that means flying up into the air and then falling down like a leaf, a pattern of leaves perhaps recognizable, consumable or renewable partly the way sand moves like water in a herringbone pattern on the skin or why you don't use music it could have been you as phantom loop, playhouse and its action the issue of recognizability flashing in the foggiest notions of those little shapes outlined in blue making a fuse box for false light falling on a face restoring the shadow of a shadowed foot, small things, eyelashes

THE LAWS

of noise and time, laws of instead of. Whose traffic jam is whose? If you open that window an alarm goes off. A minimum of energy is required to maintain the folded state. You agree for once, the three-dimensional folded pattern is not conclusion-driven. Your reaction to this redness is not indecent. What we're all trying to do is clear a space or feel that idea. From the social angle, the air is full of red-hot life-vests. The origins of the doctrine, it seems, are very ancient. First moment I taste you it's the groping seeking agreement.

How's this, the illustrated version: the plane was going down into gray chop, its belly about to scrape along the shoal of black lava rock, where it would finally stop, teetering precariously, half in the water, your hands half around my waist? The smallest possible energy to dislodge your concern was the leak in the manifold. That you could live with an increase of temperature, in another time, full of salt, crossed with the other's formula.

The other music was enormous rotating blades. Cultural bodies piled on the back of straight-backed chairs began to melt or move. For example, the red jacket or redingote sporting flashy buttons. Auditions for the echo were taking place on the charred upper floor of the library. In both cases, the random coil of memory, the heat, the scent of ripe peaches on trees growing in a ditch that had been a moat protecting the fortress protecting the island.

In the window, a pile of boulders, mountains blocking the view of what? In any case, the haunting takes place in a forest, memory occurs in the present. Ideally, their bodies, the ocean, flat, white and full of facts.

PORTUGUESE ROSE, WINTER'S ROSE

I want a heart-shaped coffin, said
the song, a guitar shape how it
happens a person comes to the door
and says work makes the space where

we live a contraction of time
not to be seen is to be dead. Light
on a hand waving light on a
face is our witness at

moments unable to look directly
at a single word to see or say
what things are broth

spilled on the table or
the truth of winter not to be
seen is to be dead.

ARTIFICIAL MEMORY 7

On the freeway that day a huge horse replaced the engine of the earthmover. Who could calibrate the horse's power? The traffic was thick. In my convertible, I could feel the heat coming off the horse's body. Each hoof was the size of my head. Vehicles lined up in front and behind. The horse-drawn equipment was on my left. At every step, the horse lifted a hoof to the level of my shoulder. Traffic was coming up fast on the right and whizzing down off the ramp just ahead.

ARTIFICIAL MEMORY 9

This is the image of effort. This is an image of two individuals, singularities, particularities, under the influence of impulse, the impulse in this case to have a conversation or disturbance of ideas about a common topic or object. They must discover what of the subject or topic is common to them, although at first that seems obvious, it's a rhyming relationship. The idea of stretching time is in the form.

FOR SHADE

There are simply tons of clouds

not-of-this-world
                during the dream
Love it when it is lovely

Please reconfirm many times
the salt flowers just forming
on the surface of the water

Please reconfirm many times
it was as we imagined the
CIA selling to children

Night falls as it did on the
                original language
The parade went by but we
didn't see it or the sound
of the parade appeared

they disappeared
Now the woman lives alone. And
what does she do while alone? She
lives

its uncommon austerity
dreamlike not in the sense of
being vague but
rather in its clarity and vividness
coupled with its

not to mention how many
suffering to fund them new story
or near story "protect your thoughts"

DESIRE AND ITS DOUBLE

From pyro to bio feel forward
ahead of a series of breakfasts
sumptuous, opulent intention

Coffee and hot milk, bread, butter,
cellophane packets of jam, purple
and orange pouring out of the hole

In her favor to ask, piece by piece
in passing, another, a hanging
the Christmas cactus is flowering

How could they not have noticed
those "little bits of wood"
become the body of a boat?

Water the apparatus undraped
how much physics can be
patented by the human body

Suppose the moon-blind
divers compose little
shows for you in the light
in the street our blind
moon absorbing smoke
reflecting orange night

FOR ROBERT CREELEY, *Together*, 1996

THE OLYMPICS IS ALL IN YOUR MIND

FOR ELLIOT ANDERSON

bluish-white, scarce ore, shaking and red splotches as if her leg was all bloody and then blood would drip on the rug and on the chair calming, like a color, like blue, or calming like the pink of a child's room or a hospital corridor, pink pearl or a kind of peach color intending to be calming like the absence of discourse
you simply keep going as the shadows get long, twos and then threes and sixes until finally two enter(s) and one last one
but then some tentative foot placements, as if the floor was suddenly hot or covered with a fine layer of ground glass, fine as a powder imagine the dancers to be in the room, in the room with the blue chair and blue air, sheet music strewn about

■

They left a long time ago.
Strides into the room.
Strides in this restricted space?
Stepped then, gingerly more likely. Entered gently, tentatively, stepping between the coffee table strewn with papers, possibly pages of

street music, I mean sheet music, drafts or sketches of an unfinished piece, as yet untitled, sporadically thought and partially remembered. Steps between the upholstered blue chair and the coffee table strewn with papers, then past the blue chair filled with blue air, appearing to aim for the sofa on the opposite side of the room, outside the frame. Debates about suing a rhetorical device, perhaps repetition or receptor theory, with variations, here, but lets the idea slip away out of the frame, over the falls in a barrel.

People were still pulling that prank over fifty years ago, before the beginning of her reign. The idea of her reign over a barrel over the falls.

■

The one not in the room at that time had been trying to organize an event, a spectacle patterned after his idea of the olympics as they once were. Nothing like the corporate sports events of today but rather more like an imagination of the *arche*, sports, arts, *arete*, competition and excellence, risk. This time they would be in a town he'd visited in Mexico. Or in Paris, in and around an abandoned automobile factory. With corporate sponsorship, or at least seed money. Tennis and Theater. What he enjoyed. What he enjoyed watching on the television, also outside the frame, in that room, from the couch or the upholstered blue chair, during the afternoon with the curtains drawn against the light like the light now, leaching out the color, the substance, the very forms from the room. Drafts of the proposal were piled uncollated on the coffee table near the blue inflatable chair. How to approach potential subscribers, he wondered.

■

Did she know that painting whose title was the same as her book? There is no evidence of painting or even books about painting in that room, only mirrors and, at times, smoke.

They hadn't been all the way through the argument about meaning. There might be examples, if individuals could be said to be examples, not of their gibberish, for that gibberish is something else, something they own and use to fill the room's vacancy with vacancy. But their lives are maps, they're rather the evidence of the rupture, both collusion and opportunism, homeostatic like the blue air, like the atmosphere in the room, the way it refers—it's a stretch—to the dream of B's double room, preposterously, providing documentation, occasional, posthumous but enduring, that is the hook.

When need or pleasure being mutually addressed, erase the surface indicators of favor, the power index

■

Nothing yet said about the place mat or the dark part of the chair back facing the desk, facing the wrinkled picture plane.

A young man placed his hands on my head, along the sides of my head and said come back in six days. I said I couldn't, or thought I couldn't. He thought, come back when you can. He gave me a turquoise umbrella when I left the room. It matched the chair. It might have been behind the chair.

The black suitcase is stored behind that chair. It looks identical to the one with writing all over it, Tibetan writing in white, like shoe polish, the liquid white shoe polish that comes in a plastic bottle with a sponge at the opening, under the cap, so you can brush the polish onto your white canvas shoes or white leather shoes once you've lifted them from under the other chair.

THE CATASTROPHE

This is strange tongue in the form of a heart where atoms of color dance, colors of manifestations on the soft ground of conscience. This is an illustrated fish, a little blue fork or prongs as incarnations. This is a bucket of energy, a barred spiral. This sand bar permits the passage of blood with variations, horizontal. Light. This light is on a dark blue ground or a deep red ground or a midnight green ground, a disk of dancing metal arrows, all show. Ruling colors of the spiral, precipitous, terrifying, an ancient treaty. Give up the idea of the state. Can it be said? To whom can it be said? To someone's father or mother? The world, night, demolition of homes, control of water. Lack of water. Build and destroy. Trial. Walls of the moat or the room, their design and multiplication, constant dialogue of light and shade. Narrow verticals. Rise. All rise. Rare and free. Or rather free. A little free. An image of redefining, explicit, the point of the arrow, head down. Twice the energy. Little known and less represented. Observed in various visible forms, clarity, display. Evolving. The many. The tongue as haptic form evoking that principle.

IN MEMORIAM JACQUES DERRIDA

There is no Waste Land. —JESSIE L. WESTON

Monkeys!?! Are they all
monkeys?
Tired monkeys.

D'you know that during the rococo
period
       —of the eighteenth century
you monkeys were given a new
identity by representing the
exoticism of the Far East
       —I would fain hope . . .

Verily, kiddo, I walk
among monkeys as among
the foreskins and limbs
of monkeys—monkeys
in ruins.

gala or apocalypse,
apocalypse or

a part of the body, a
secret part

But let's go for a moment to
the great ecumenical current
the discovery or the great
unveiling—I kid you not—
the ear whispering under its veil of hair—
or the milky way—study the tone
itself—

(I kid you not) the clock
chimes midnight—bong bong bong etc.
what changes a tone, what
causes a rupture of tone? How
does one distinguish—

He was just starting to get to the
Heideggerian conjugation of the
personal. La! Re-signing himself.

Come, come.

Then his
signature will have taken place.

His signature has
taken place.
Monkeys—love 'em or leave 'em.

DEAR ROBERT,

    Hi, just wanted to check in
with you, see what's happening. I
was reading your "ACHILLES' SONG,"
the first poem in *GROUNDWORK:*
Before the War in which Thetis
promises Achilles not a boat
but the mirage of a boat. There is
always a "before the war," isn't
there? Some war. Another war.
Miss you.
        Love,

        Norma

P.S. and back of that war
"the deeper unsatisfied war"

SARABANDE

"and then looks at
the stars" from the
bed in the ambulance

looks up at boughs of
trees shifting quickly
lit in blackness

blackening soft, deep
siren's song—she died
several times that night

and only in the weeks
to come started and
started to come back

then forward which is
real life

WATER IS BEST

Here from the tap the heart beats
to the talk, bleeds the order can
never be discovered in the red
past hay (harvest) in Poison Town

where the action takes place—the
Shah etc.—the President etc.—bending
down now trying to pick things up
pretending to read where to read

is to misunderstand hearts and pipes
the fiction of everyday life, a glass
of water with or without ice

NANO-SHADES

the male deliberately positions himself
over his lover's fangs

the key is gravity
blankets, personal items

and clothing, extra-solar planets (class M)
like our sun, the memory

of history, empty or full
scared the daylights out of the name

LIKE FIRES

Like wasps' nests
where we were

like many fires buildings
crumpling in flames in a

forest of trucks rushing
past in the night, headlights

blazing
To see, hand

covering her eyes, hand
brushing back his hair, the sounds

of forest days and night
sounds sun comes up or is

obscured by clouds or it is
raining or blazing light is it

late, too late for me to
come back to your place

LEAVING THE GARDENS OF ETERNITY

Spiral galaxies were expanding
at the center of nothing
complication swinging

from the other side
"I can't control my soldiers," said
the Congolese government officer

pigeons on the other balcony
examine minerals and tears (alarms)
guess what: you can sit at the table

and watch—hello stranger—
the man was kicking a horse
then the man fell down

THE STATIONMASTER

Pluto stands in the dark and
thinks

between the sky overhead directly
and dead anger

all bedrock, brutal and
puritanical

dance to the fire station of
faith

create deafness, come
taste

FROM "IN OUR OWN BACKYARD"

You can't image what it's like here. In her past
life, she was a clandestine operator in ancient
Egypt. In a past life she had her heart ripped out,
ritual sacrifice. We all know what that
means, right, to have your heart ripped out. Torn
from the body, one's "own" body, alive and torn.

The unspeaking speaker. The man coughs.
Orientation. Two bells, a motorcar on the
street, on-lookers. H22-3416. Men, maybe
four, inside. Vast numbers of people, faces
turned to the east. Four nurses holding four
swaddled babes, four bottles.

Six men walking forward on a country road
all wearing suits, coats, vests and ties. Upon
his shoulders, one of the men carries a man with
no legs. The man with no legs is wearing a

bathrobe. In a landscape a train passes from
top right to bottom left. People are packed inside
as well as on the roof and holding on at the sides.

One man, naked, his back turned to the
window, light on inside. A bird in a cage hung
on a hook at the top left-hand corner of the
window. A man in profile to the left, eyes closed
mouth open wide, singing. Or thought he was
singing. He did. Or we did. The back of a chair and
three tall mirrors. At their focal point a woman
stands, arms akimbo. She's wearing evening dress
black high heels, long white gown, long black
gloves, necklace, earrings.

Outside the bakery, a horse-drawn hearse
approaches. A woman in an apron tests green grapes
eating them before placing bunches in a wooden
crate. Inside a Quonset hut, there's a long
table with men sitting in chairs writing or paying
attention to one man standing at the table, hands

in the pockets of his jumpsuit. Shirtless men seated on the floor, some on towels or blankets, are doing exercises. Friday afternoon, cold grim day. We meet in the museum, at a picture called "Birmingham."

Sign on exterior wall saying "WELCOME."

ABOUT THE AUTHOR

Born in Toronto, Canada, Norma Cole received an MA in French from
the University of Toronto in 1967, moving to France in time to absorb
the revolutionary atmosphere of the May '68 general strike. Returning
to Toronto in the early '70s, she migrated to San Francisco in 1977,
where she has lived ever since. A member of the circle of poets around
Robert Duncan in the '80s, and a fellow traveler of San Francisco's
language poets, Cole is also allied with contemporary French poets like
Jacques Roubaud, Claude Royet-Journoud, and Emmanuel Hocquard.
She is a prolific French translator and has taught at many schools,
including the University of San Francisco and San Francisco State.
During winter 2004/05, Cole could be seen inhabiting a 1950s living
room as part of the California Historical Society's *Collective Memory*
installation series. More recently, she curated a show by Marina Adams
at the Cue Arts Foundation in NYC. Cole has been the recipient of a
Wallace Alexander Gerbode Foundation Award, Gertrude Stein Awards,
the Fund for Poetry, and the Foundation for Contemporary Arts.

The state of the world calls out for poetry to save it. LAWRENCE FERLINGHETTI

CITY LIGHTS SPOTLIGHT SHINES A LIGHT ON THE WEALTH OF INNOVATIVE AMERICAN POETRY BEING WRITTEN TODAY. WE PUBLISH ACCOMPLISHED FIGURES KNOWN IN THE POETRY COMMUNITY AS WELL AS YOUNG EMERGING POETS, USING THE CULTURAL VISIBILITY OF CITY LIGHTS TO BRING THEIR WORK TO A WIDER AUDIENCE. IN DOING SO, WE ALSO HOPE TO DRAW ATTENTION TO THOSE SMALL PRESSES PUBLISHING SUCH AUTHORS. WITH CITY LIGHTS SPOTLIGHT, WE WILL MAINTAIN OUR STANDARD OF INNOVATION AND INCLUSIVENESS BY PUBLISHING HIGHLY ORIGINAL POETRY FROM ACROSS THE CULTURAL SPECTRUM, REFLECTING OUR LONGSTANDING COMMITMENT TO THIS MOST ANCIENT AND STUBBORNLY ENDURING FORM OF ART.

CITY LIGHTS SPOTLIGHT

1

Norma Cole, *Where Shadows Will:*
Selected Poems 1988-2008

2

Anselm Berrigan, *Free Cell*

3

Andrew Joron, *Trance Archive:*
New and Selected Poems

4

Cedar Sigo, *Stranger in Town*

5

Will Alexander, *Compression & Purity*

6

Micah Ballard, *Waifs and Strays*

7

Julian Talamantez Brolaski, *Advice for Lovers*